WHY STRAIGHT GUYS
LOVE THEIR GAY GUYS

REVIVING THE ROOTS
OF MALE SEXUALITY

Also by David Dalton

Fugue in Ursa Major (2014)
Oratorio in Ursa Major (2016)
Symphony in Ursa Major (2018)

The Ursa Major series is a science
fiction series which applies the
imagination to many of the themes
discussed in this book.

Why Straight Guys Love Their Gay Guys

Reviving the Roots of Male Sexuality

David Dalton

ACORN ABBEY

Published 2017 by Acorn Abbey Books

Madison, North Carolina

ISBN 978-0-9916132-9-8

Acorn Abbey Books Madison, North Carolina
acornabbey.com
PRCS00000000

Contents

∽ 1 ∾

The manifesto

On March 2, 2017, Huffington Post's Highline carried a beautifully researched but depressing piece by Michael Hobbes on the state of gay men. The article, "Together Alone: The Epidemic of Gay Loneliness," rounds up the mounting evidence that gay men, in spite of our remarkable progress in the past fifty years, have not gotten any healthier or any happier. But the question remains: Why? Something remains badly wrong. What?

Hobbes' article does not focus on the questions of why and what. Rather, Hobbes looks at surveys of mental health, suicide rates, life expectancy, measures of stress, measures of physical health, and rates of

addiction and substance abuse. Hobbes also inter-
views gay men who are dealing with these issues. Their
heartbreaking testimony is a wakeup call. Obviously,
much work remains to be done, in spite of the progress
we have made. But not only do we not have a diagnosis
of what might be wrong, we no longer seem to have a
goal for further progress.

In case you haven't yet read Hobbes' article, here are
some highlights, with snippets of Hobbes' article in
italics:

*The rates of depression, loneliness and substance abuse
in the gay community remain stuck in the same place
they've been for decades. Gay people are now, depending
on the study, between 2 and 10 times more likely than
straight people to take their own lives. We're twice as
likely to have a major depressive episode. And just like
the last epidemic we lived through, the trauma appears
to be concentrated among men. In a survey of gay men
who recently arrived in New York City, three-quarters
suffered from anxiety or depression, abused drugs or
alcohol or were having risky sex — or some combination
of the three. Despite all the talk of our "chosen families,"
gay men have fewer close friends than straight people or
gay women.*

Hobbes points out that this is not just an American
problem:

In the Netherlands, where gay marriage has been legal since 2001, gay men remain three times more likely to suffer from a mood disorder than straight men, and 10 times more likely to engage in "suicidal self-harm." In Sweden, which has had civil unions since 1995 and full marriage since 2009, men married to men have triple the suicide rate of men married to women.

The overall health of gay men is at risk:

Gay men everywhere, at every age, have higher rates of cardiovascular disease, cancer, incontinence, erectile dysfunction, allergies and asthma.

Our gay communities may actually drag us down rather than support us:

For other minority groups, living in a community with people like them is linked to lower rates of anxiety and depression. It helps to be close to people who instinctively understand you. But for us, the effect is the opposite. Several studies have found that living in gay neighborhoods predicts higher rates of risky sex and meth use and less time spent on other community activities like volunteering or playing sports. A 2009 study suggested that gay men who were more linked to the gay community were less satisfied with their own romantic relationships....

"[I]n-group discrimination" does more harm to your

psyche than getting rejected by members of the majority. It's easy to ignore, roll your eyes and put a middle finger up to straight people who don't like you because, whatever, you don't need their approval anyway. Rejection from other gay people, though, feels like losing your only way of making friends and finding love. Being pushed away from your own people hurts more because you need them more.

Feminine men are devalued and stigmatized, and most gay men say that they want to date someone masculine:

These masculinity norms exert a toll on everyone, even their perpetrators. Feminine gay men are at higher risk of suicide, loneliness and mental illness. Masculine gay men, for their part, are more anxious, have more risky sex and use drugs and tobacco with greater frequency.

Inside all this bad news are at least three important clues to the roots of our problem.

The first clue is that our gay communities don't seem to make us better off. Instead, living in places such as San Francisco's Castro district may actually amplify the damage. The second clue is our unsatisfied hunger for masculinity. The third clue is that gay marriage has not helped.

In this book, we'll try to follow these clues.

Many gay people seemed to assume that, once we had gay marriage, we'd have it all. But after gay marriage became a reality, suddenly we all went quiet, waiting for the dawn of a utopia that has not come. It's as though we're embarrassed to admit to ourselves — or to the rest of society — that gay marriage has not solved our problems. Hobbes' article shows that gay marriage hasn't made a dent in the measures of our well-being.

Many people did not notice that the idea of gay marriage — radical as it was — actually was an idea developed by gay conservatives. It was gay conservatives such Andrew Sullivan, Jonathan Rauch, Bruce Bawer, and others whose names are less well known who developed the arguments for gay marriage and the strategy for making gay marriage legal. We owe those conservatives an enormous debt. Gay marriage is a huge achievement in equality and equal justice. It's a major landmark in gay history. I know many of the conservative gay men to whom we owe the right to marriage. Jonathan Rauch is an old friend. Still, their goals were conservative goals — getting gay men to settle down and take care of each other, making us more acceptable to — and more like — straight society, for example. Gay marriage, they believed, would tame us, contain us, and integrate us into society in ways that would be good for everyone. Indeed gay people and our rights are more accepted now than gay men — whether conservative or leftist — would have dared to imagine a few decades ago. The conservative idea of gay marriage — an idea that originated in the mid-1990s — was a reaction to radical gay politics of the left (identity politics), which was then ascendant. Now radical gay leftists have almost vanished from the scene. Frankly, I miss them, though they were sometimes wrong (as gay conservatives have sometimes been wrong). But my point here is that neither leftist nor right-leaning gay activists have come up with any ideas that have brought gay men any closer to the Promised Land. As for what comes next, both right and left are out of ideas.

So, with no diagnosis of what's wrong with the lives of gay men and no vision of what to do about it, we must be missing something that is very important. But what? Is it possible that what we're missing has been right under our noses all along? I think it has. But it's fiercely forbidden and remains out of our reach — for now.

Though I am well aware that, scientifically, we still don't have a noncontroversial picture of how and for what reasons nature makes some of us gay, nevertheless I believe that we now know enough to draw some conclusions. (I just used the word "nature," though I also recognize that many things are socially constructed. We'll get to that.) And by the way, this book is primarily addressed to gay and straight men, though some of it also applies to lesbians. We gay men just don't fit the world that we all now live in. We used to fit (something that we've mostly forgotten), but now we don't. A reasonably clear picture of our predicament emerges if we combine what we know from anthropology, evolutionary psychology, and the records left to us by older cultures including the Greeks.

This picture, unfortunately, is not a picture that is going to make us happier any time soon. That's because the problem isn't with gay men, and it's not something that we gay men can fix on our own. Queer theory cannot help us with this. The problem is with the kind of cultures that we've all — gay and straight — had to live in since the end of the pagan era. Our present sexual environment has been poisoned by a sharp break from human history and by radical, artificial changes in the social environment. The new rules are not based on nature or on naturally arising social constructions. Instead, the new rules are based on unnatural and artificial propositions that were conjured out of thin air in the minds of theologians. In short, it was religion that did this to us.

Human instincts and sexualities evolved, naturally, over thousands of years in tribal societies. There are a number of books that you can turn to on this subject. One popular book is *Sex at Dawn*. I'll mention other sources in the next chapter, the chapter on what we can learn from anthropology. Sure, the subject is controversial. Sex and sexualities are always controversial now. But that our human origins are in hunter-gatherer tribes is not controversial. The important thing is that gay sexualities arose — we could even say evolved — in tribes in which people needed each other. The size of a tribe varied, but imagine a tribe of fifty to one hundred people or so.

If you assume that gay males are about 2 percent of the male population, then you would expect to find one or two of us in a tribe that size. (For the purposes of my argument, there is no need to debate the actual percentage.) If you further assume that gay males were reasonably happy in hunter-gatherer tribes and that they were having sex (wasn't everybody?), then whom do you suppose they were having sex with? There can be only one answer. They were having sex with the other 98 percent of the men. We'll talk more about this in the next chapter, on anthropology.

This idea of "gay" men having sex with "straight" men is condemned so harshly in our time (by both gay people and by straight people) that it's difficult for us to see that, not only is easy male-male sex (for all males, not just gay males) our history and our birthright, but also that it must be our future, if our future is to be a happier one. Straight males are our forbidden fruit. They are what we are missing. They are what we used to have. They are the source of the masculinity that we gay men crave. And our gay ghettoes are precisely the places where straight men are the scarcest. It's no wonder that our gay ghettoes don't make us any happier.

It was Christian theologians (Augustine of Hippo, in particular, 354-430 A.D.) who codified the forbidding. Though the pagan Greeks and Romans developed the idea of one-man one-woman marriage, marriage was mostly a legal and social arrangement then, not so much a sexual one. The Greeks and Romans understood quite well that men liked to have sex with each other. There was no theological difficulty or stigma for the pagans, because Christianity had not yet appeared. The pagan gods had the same kind of sex that humans had (and sometimes the gods had sex *with* humans). Yes, there were pagans such as the stoics who saw sex as a distraction from nobler pursuits, but the stoics never had (or wanted) anything like the vast machinery of repression and cultural genocide that Christian theologians and authoritarians built.

Because my ancestry is Irish, I find the sexual history of the Celts particularly fascinating. The Celts were among the first to be brutalized by the methods that Christians developed to try to stamp out homosexuality and the cultures in which male-male sex was normal. One wishes that we knew more about the Celts (their suppression by the Romans and Christians was in many ways a genocide), but we do know, if we can believe some early historians (for example, Strabo, Athenaeus, and Diodorus) that Celtic warriors were so open and enthusiastic about male-male sex that even the Greeks found the Celts' male sexualities remarkable. Many would agree that lots of male-male sex was pretty much the way things were throughout the pagan world. The classical pagan cultures, advanced as some of them became, seem to have retained their connections to the naturally exuberant male sexualities of our paleolithic tribal ancestors. The classical pagans knew how to harness those male-male bonds for social and military value (think Athens and Thebes). How, then, did we gay males come to be so miserable, so hated, and to have such unhappy sex lives? (I foresee some resistance here from some of you informing me how happy your sex life is with your gay boyfriend or husband. Good for you! But most of us are not so lucky.)

It's not that the natural sexual arrangements of the tribal and pagan cultures faded away because guys lost interest in having sex with each other. It's that natural sexualities were systematically crushed by new forms of sexual repression based on radical new theologies. (See *From Shame to Sin: The Christian Transformation of Sexual Morality in Late Antiquity*, by Kyle Harper, Harvard University Press, 2013.) The centuries-long work of this crushing, of course, was done by the church, buttressed in its early years by the coercive authority of the Roman state. Once this repression was established and internalized, and once older arrangements were forgotten, ordinary people actually began to internalize and enforce the repression against themselves. They taught it to their children. We still do.

It's hard for me to understand why homosexuality was so threatening to early Christian theologians. They thought it was "unnatural" (Augustine of Hippo). Perhaps homosexuality was threatening because it was such a prominent feature of paganism, and the church's intention was to exterminate paganism. The church-state structure became obsessed with suppressing male-male sexuality even as male-male sexuality went underground in the church and its monasteries. Sex-spooked authoritarians remain obsessed today. You don't waste water where there is no fire to put out. And you don't waste so much effort on sexual repression where there is nothing to repress. The intensity and cruelty of the church's repression of the Celtic cultures of western Europe are well documented in history, though of course that history is presented as the church's triumph in bringing salvation to the godless heathens and barbarians. That history was repeated when European cultures "discovered" the Americas, Africa, and Asia and began to colonize those places and send in the missionaries. Were it not for the church's repression, I think it's clear that our sex lives today would be very different — all of our sex lives, not just the sex lives of gay men. It was the church and its theologies that broke the continuity between ourselves and our tribal and pagan ancestors. That, I believe, is what led to our sexual misery today. It was not moral progress. It was a moral catastrophe.

Our sexualities are perfectly natural, and that is defense enough. E.O. Wilson, the eminent biologist, has described mechanisms whereby nature could have evolved gay people, for reasons that we don't yet fully understand: "[H]omosexuality may give advantages to the group by special talents, unusual qualities of personality, and the specialized roles and professions it generates. There is abundant evidence that such is the case in both preliterate and modern societies.... A society that condemns homosexuality harms itself." [*The Social Conquest of Earth*, 2012]

Wilson, it happens, also is no great friend of religion and theology: "[I]t seems clear that ethical philosophy will benefit from a reconstruction of its precepts based on both science and culture. If such greater understanding amounts to the 'moral relativism' so fervently despised by the doctrinally righteous, so be it."

The mechanisms, scripts, and templates of this sexual repression — all of them with roots traceable to the church (and to patriarchal Judaism) — are all around us today. But they've become largely invisible to us because we've never known any alternatives. The mechanisms of our sexual repression are almost as invisible to us as the air we breathe.

For example, any straight man who contemplates the possibility of having sex with another man will immediately and automatically face an internalized barrier thrown up by a script:

It's contagious! If I do that, it will make me gay. It will make me less of a man. It will pollute me, make me less acceptable to women. If anybody found out, I'd be derided, devalued, and ruined. I'd better not do it because it's not worth all that.

Those are all warnings from a church that our hunter-gatherer ancestors didn't have to deal with. Yes, the Romans developed some unhealthy notions about the active-passive, top-bottom elements of sexual behavior, and those notions are still with us. But that didn't stop the pre-Christian Romans from having lots of male-male sex.

These days, if you visit any online forum where men anonymously discuss their sexual issues, one thing you'll hear again and again is something like this: "I'm straight, and my gay friend wants to suck me off. I'm tempted, because I hear they give superb blow jobs. If I let him do it, will that make me gay?"

Almost always, the answer will be: "Yes. That would make you either gay or bi." This instant classification is considered to be an open and shut case. There is little inquiry into the complexity of the sexualities involved. There is only kneejerk classification, case closed. If you argue, you will be assailed. But it's wrong. Kneejerk classification and its identity labels are no better than the efforts of queer theorists to solve all our problems with jargon. At the level of human instincts, labels and jargon have nothing to do with anything and shed no light. Occasional sex with another male will no more make a straight-identified man gay than occasional sex with women has made me straight. Sure, some men are much gayer than others, and some men are exclusively gay. But all human males are born with the wiring to enjoy male-male sex, just as they enjoy masturbation. There's a great deal of truth in an old gay joke: Question: What's the difference between a straight guy and a gay guy? Answer: Six beers.

Let's look at some more of the scripts, all of them taught and learned, that perpetuate the stigma of male-male sex:

■ A gay man is secretly in love with his straight best friend. Should he come out of the closet and petition for sex? *It would fuck up our relationship. He'll get mad at me. He might even dump me. He might tell people and embarrass me. I'd better not.*

■ A straight man is considering having sex with a gay friend. The straight man suspects he'd enjoy it. It would be kind and generous to reward his gay friend's affection and admiration. *It would fuck up our relationship. He might become a pest. Sex might be all he wants. He'd tell people and embarrass me. I'd better not.*

■ A straight woman finds out that the straight man she's dating has had sex with a man. *Dump him, and shame him appropriately in the process. He's no longer husband material.*

■ A gay man is deeply emotionally involved with a straight man. *The gay man's gay friends say, "Are you crazy? How can you waste your time on someone who can't give you what you want and who will only crush you? You know how those things always end. Pining for straight guys is internalized homophobia. Stick to your own kind."*

■ A straight man tells his straight buddies that a gay guy has fallen for him. *The straight man's friends say, "Let him know how deluded he is. Start treating him coldly. If he persists, tell him to get lost. What did you do to encourage him? Watch out for your reputation. We were starting to wonder about you, you know."*

An important point that Michael Hobbes' article "Together Alone" makes beautifully is that what gay men need is (of course!) the one thing that gay men as a group are deficient in — masculinity. (I foresee a bunch of comments informing me how masculine your boyfriend or husband is, or if he's not, how much you don't care. Good for you!) It then naturally follows that straight men are the best sources of what gay men need. That's a terrible predicament, qualitatively equivalent to blocking straight men from getting what they want from women, or women from men. Surely our gay tribal ancestors had access to the masculinity they needed from the men in their tribe. But now the rules see to it that we gay men are cut off from the one

natural resource that is *overflowing* with what we need
— the masculinity of straight men.

And just look at what being gay does to our odds. We
gay men are now, post-liberation, expected to make our
emotional living with only 2 percent (or so) of the male
population — to stick to our own kind. To try to make
something that difficult possible, we urbanize and
ghettoize and sort each other out according to degrees
of masculinity and as tops and bottoms (with tops
always in short supply, my bottom friends complain).
But that can't be how we evolved. We evolved in tribal
situations in which much more of the male population
was potentially available to us (and I've got news for
you — straight guys are not all tops, which is a bigger
problem for straight men than most people realize).
In a tribal situation, there were no urban gay ghettoes
to migrate to. This is a good thought experiment, by
the way, to present to straight people to help straight
people understand the unworkability of our gay predicament, to help them understand why gay men tend
to be so unhappy, and why so many of us kill ourselves:
What if 98 percent of the people you are attracted to
were off-limits, and you might get your bones broken
if you even try? And what if the remaining 2 percent of
your own kind, for the most part, don't have enough of
the masculinity (or femininity) that you really want?
Do you think that your average straight man or straight
woman would settle for a rotten deal like that? If such

a life were forced upon them, along with heaping helpings of scorn and condemnation, then what do you think would happen to the statistics on their health and well-being?

So how do we get out of this mess? If you can believe as I do that gay men are unhappy because theologies ruined the world for us, then it follows that there is no fix for the lives of gay men that gay men alone can bring about. Liberation didn't do it for us. Gay marriage didn't do it for us. The inconvenient truth is that our entire society would have to change (to more closely resemble the way things used to be) if we gay men are ever going to be able to live again in a world that works for us. Or to say it another way, ghettoes for the 2 percent, where gay men stick to their own kind, can never work. A solution involving segregation, ghettoization, and "liberation" just does not exist.

There may be some small causes for optimism. A 2014 article in the journal *Men and Masculinities* reported that a study done in Britain by Durham University found that 93 percent of straight males of college age had cuddled with a male friend. I have no idea whether that study has been replicated, but, if it's true, then we're on our way. The straight men in those British universities certainly make nice beefcake calendars for their gay admirers, don't they? And it makes sense that Europeans would lead the way, because they're years ahead of Americans in throwing religion off their backs.

Many gay men — especially our stalwart gay activists — are deeply invested in the idea that the gay identity is an achievement. As a necessary and temporary adaptation after centuries of post-Christian invisibility and repression, it *was* an achievement. The gay identity was an early — and necessary — step in finding our way out of the wilderness. Gay marriage, and the social acceptance and recognition of equality that gay marriage represents, was another huge achievement.

But if we want a future in which gay people can be happy, then we have a huge task ahead of us, because it's not just we gay people who will have to change. *Everybody* will have to change, gay and straight. But though everyone stands to gain, some will lose some privileges.

Women, unfortunately for them, have a privilege to lose — the privilege of monopolizing straight male sexuality. If men freely had sex with each other in older societies, then women did not have a monopoly privilege. I have no idea how women might work out that loss of privilege, though they certainly can be assured that straight men will not lose interest in them. As a gay man, I'm afraid that I have very little help to offer women on this subject, other than to suggest that women take a look at (for example) the female sexualities of the ancient Celts. I'm aware that the scholarship on the status of women in Celtic societies is considered inconclusive. Nevertheless it's an area that has inspired the feminist imagination, as it inspires my gay imagination.

As for men, men have much to gain. Once men learn (as tribal men must have known) that male-male sex doesn't devalue them, doesn't emasculate them, and doesn't force a whole new unwelcome identity on them, then look at what they get: eager no-strings sex, sexual variety, better bonding, a superb alternative to masturbation, superior blow jobs, and a form of appreciation and admiration that they probably haven't been getting. Gay men will worship them and make them feel like gods, not just get them off. Every gay man deserves a calendar guy.

During my long life, I have had several enduring and loving relationships with straight men, as well as with gay men. One such relationship with a straight man, which was not sexual (though I wanted it), lasted 25 years before a new wife obliged him to dump me. Another such relationship, which was very sexual, lasted nine years before a new wife obliged him to dump me. Another such relationship has been going for eight years now, and so far I have not been dumped (though like so many gay men I am irrationally predisposed to always being braced for rejection, and I'm always getting backgrounded by the monopoly privileges of women and by the fact that straight men are, well, straight).

Though I am scarred and damaged (what gay man

isn't?), somehow I have escaped the worst of the problems that afflict gay men. I am not an alcoholic, I have never used dangerous drugs, I've been in therapy only once (midlife crisis), my health is superb, I don't think about suicide, and I have never been a sex addict. In fact, I lived in San Francisco for 18 years without ever going to a gay bar or bath. And for nine of those 18 years I was having regular sex — very good sex — with a very hot and masculine straight-identified man who at the time was not married.

As with so many gay men, my gay exes have become part of my family. My first gay ex and I have known each other for almost fifty years. In my gay family, we have our share of alcoholism, HIV, histories of being bullied, serious fag bashing, depression, and early death. But we've also accomplished a hell of a lot. Careers flourished. Ph.D.'s got earned. Books got written. We've supported each other reasonably well over the years, though there also have been times when we've been mean to each other.

And I can say this. When I have loved straight men, it came to calamity only when those theological scripts were used to defeat me. The scripts dictate that, when a woman is married to a man, that man cannot have a male lover. I also know that the end of those relationships hurt the straight man as much as it hurt me. *Straight men love their gay guys.* I believe that loving both gay men and straight men somehow stabilized my life as a gay man, like the third leg of a stool, though nothing has ever been easy. The three legs of the stool, in my experience, are: 1. Self-respect 2. Gay friends and lovers, and 3. Straight friends and lovers. That three-legged stool is ancient. The church sawed off two of the legs. The horrible strain of that broke the first leg, our self-respect. Gay pride and gay marriage have done much to restore the second leg — the gay friends and lovers in our lives — and the first leg, our self-respect. But we won't be able to fix the third leg — straight friends and lovers — until we go back to nature and integrate gay sexuality not only with male sexuality in general but with human sexuality in general. Gay sexuality is a part of male sexuality. Denying that, and cruelly suppressing it, has been disastrous for all of us.

Though it's an essay for another day, I am inclined to believe that marriage, gay or straight — except for a minority who are truly suited for marriage, and with the understanding that marriage equality is a good thing — is part of the problem, not part of the solution. Conservatives, of course — including gay conservatives — want to harness our sexualities for social goods, such as "settling men down," or getting people to commit to taking care of each other and their children. That was part of the conservative argument for gay marriage. But damming up and rechanneling a torrent as wild and as natural as male sexuality comes with a cost (paid in misery) that many of us (those who have survived, anyway) are tired of paying. Must we imagine that, in tribal societies, people *did not* get taken care of, just because men had lots of sex with each other? Who hatched the idea that sex is so dangerous? Surely societies don't necessarily fall apart just because people's sexualities are not rigorously repressed and rechanneled. The opposite may be more true. Surely happiness matters.

Let's also not forget that gay marriage is a kind of ghetto that restricts us to our own kind — 2 percent of the population. Gay marriage doesn't integrate us into the human population. It's more like a firewall. Gay marriage has not solved the problem of gay wellbeing, and it never will.

I am calling for nothing less than a rebellion against an unnatural system of sexual repression that has been used against us — against all of us — for almost two thousand years. Let's take back the word "natural," which theologians such as Augustine of Hippo used against us in claiming that what we want is "unnatural" — a fine and ancient example of the authoritarian lie that "war is peace and freedom is slavery." We owe a huge debt to the gay liberators who preceded us — to the Franklin Kamenys, to the Harvey Milks, to the authors of gay marriage, to all who have fought in the trenches for justice and equality. But we are still living in an unnatural world with a grossly unfair and unjust system of sexual "morality."

Fifty years ago, it was clear what injustices we were fighting against. We were fighting injustices including sodomy laws, harassment, and the lies about who we are. Then we had a new goal: gay marriage. Today it is not so clear what we are fighting for. We don't know what's holding us back. We aren't even talking about it anymore. I believe that what is holding us back is invisible razor wire — theological, cultural, internalized and disguised — that contains us. It surrounds *all* of us, not just those of us who are gay. Without our really being aware of it, this invisible razor wire limits what we do, what we feel, and what we think pretty much every hour of every day, as was intended by the authoritarians who worked for centuries to put that system of razor wire in place. Politics, Washington, and the courts have done for us as much as politics, Washington, and the courts can do. The sodomy laws are gone, and gay marriage is now the law of the land. What matters now is how bold we are in how we dare to live our lives.

When it comes to sex, people — especially repressed people — are always sneaky. What I'm proposing involves more sneakiness, at least for a while. But let's call it privacy instead of sneakiness. Living boldly involves widening our raids outside the reservations into which our gay sexualities have been herded and confined. Our gay ghettos were never much of an achievement or a refuge. They were reservations into which our sexualities were quarantined, reservations plagued with the same health-destroying and soul-suffocating problems as any reservation or place of incarceration. We'll have begun the work when we venture out of our gay ghettos, delete our gay apps, and assert that we are *men* with a man's complex sexuality — not just gay men with a cramped and strangely unsatisfying gay sexuality. We venture off the reservation to bestow and to expand, not to acquire or to forbid. We assert that our sexualities are a natural right, a human right. We condemn (and make fun of) abstract repressive theologies, which do not serve us — either in this world or the next. We'll have begun the work when no one gets unearned privileges that are denied to others. We'll have begun the work when straight men start to realize that nature meant us gay guys for them, and when straight men start getting used to our admiration and *liking* the way it expands their horizons and their liberties. There is no need to rub people's noses in what we do in our raids outside the reservation, or to post pictures of it in social media. Rather, just *do* it, in secret as necessary, and come out of the closet another day, after we've emptied the reservations.

Or, look at it this way. Nature saw to it that there's more than enough masculinity and enough men in the world to go around. In fact, women often complain that there's *too much* loose masculinity discharged into the world where it's not wanted (which ought to be a clue that something is wrong inside the razor wire). But we gay guys are not getting the fair share of male attention and masculinity that nature wired us for and that we need in order to feel completed and happy. We gay guys are a part of nature's ecological balance. All human beings need masculinity in their lives — men, women, and children. If nature didn't equip you to make enough masculinity on your own, then you make a deal to acquire it from someone, the way women do.

We gay guys will negotiate a fair deal for the masculinity that we need and aren't getting, and we have plenty of virtues and assets to trade for it. Even the least rich, least attractive, least masculine and least artistically gifted gay guys can deliver superior blow jobs. But let's be done with the theologies that for 2,000 years have worked to completely shut us gay guys out of the market for the masculinity we need.

Let's stop settling for 2 percent of the pie. Let's cut the razor wire. Let's quit the reservations. Let's have it all.

∾ 2 ∾

The anthropology

Those who are heavily invested in terminology and queer theory may protest that it is wrong of me to apply words such as "gay" and "straight" to men who lived long before these identities were invented. But I would argue that men whom we would identify as gay, because they occur naturally, are recognizable across all cultures. Those who are heavily invested in categorization and identity may protest that I should not use the word "straight" for any man who has had even one sexual experience with another male. But I would argue that we all get to choose our identities. If a man chooses to self-identify as straight, then that's enough for me. For convenience, I will continue to use the terms "gay" and "straight."

In the previous section, I mentioned the book *Sex at Dawn* by Christopher Ryan and Cacilda Jethá. This was a popular book as opposed to an academic book. It made the New York Times best-seller list six weeks after publication. The book is more concerned with heterosexuality and mating than with male-male sexuality, but the book does make clear just how unnatural our notions about sexual morality are. Dan Savage, the sex advice columnist, called *Sex at Dawn* the most important book on human sexuality since Alfred Kinsey released *Sexual Behavior in the Human Male* in 1948.

Just as with Kinsey's book, *Sex at Dawn* was met with a great outcry from those who wish to preserve our culture of sexual repression, those who think that it's dangerous to mess with the status quo. An Amazon reviewer identified as "Preachereast" wrote: "It was just dumb, I would not tell anyone to pay a penny for it. The author tried to say we are like animals. We are not alley cats, we have more to us than that." The book even inspired an angry and thoroughly amateurish riposte in book form, *Sex at Dusk.*

Many people feel very threatened by challenges to the sexual status quo, especially where homosexuality and heterosexual marriage are concerned. The "defense" of heterosexual marriage became almost hysterical as gay marriage spread rapidly from state to state. Some people also feel demeaned when human sexuality is compared with animal sexuality, especially since many of those people don't believe in evolution in the first place. Just as some gay people see the gay identity as progress and as an achievement to be preserved and defended, so some people see monogamy and heterosexual marriage as progress and achievement. Today we glorify the nuclear family, having made it the only option for raising children. But in our ignorance of our origins we forget what we destroyed and what the nuclear family replaced — extended families, tribal arrangements, and fosterage systems such as that of the Celts. During most of human history, and as late as the Iron Age, units of economic cooperation (and hence the rearing of children) were larger than the nuclear family. See David L. Clarke's *Models in Archeology*, in which he uses archeology to analyze the units of economic cooperation.

We must set aside for the moment all these notions of human progress (which I don't see as progress at all), along with our squeamishness about comparing ourselves with animals. If we want to understand our instinctive sexualities, then we must look at the anthropology. Let's also keep in mind that homosexuality in pre-Christian societies occurred as only one component of complete social systems, systems that included heterosexuality, economic units, and the care of children. It was these entire systems that have been tampered with and lost, not just attitudes toward homosexuality. It follows that, if we want to imagine a future in which gay people can thrive, then we must think about our entire social systems, not just the treatment of homosexuality.

James Neill, in *The Origins and Role of Same-Sex Relations in Human Societies*, begins his story with animal sexuality, in which homosexuality is far more common than even such books as *Sex at Dawn* let on. For example, in giraffes, male-male homosexual behavior is more common than heterosexual behavior. Neill writes: "In one study in Africa, same-sex mountings among males accounted for 94 percent of all observed sexual behavior."

But having established that homosexual behavior is entirely natural and is very common in the animal kingdom, let's move on to human beings. It's the arrangements of our ancestors that interest me much more. What we find is consistent across multiple cultures, from paleolithic hunter-gatherers to the Iron Age contemporaries of classical Greece and Rome.

Neill writes:

It is apparent that before the introduction of Western sexual morality, homosexuality in one form or another seems to have been virtually universal among the tribal cultures of the aboriginal lands colonized by European explorers. Not only is homosexual behavior nearly always present among primitive cultures, but the striking similarity of the patterns in which it appears over a broad variety of peoples suggests that the forms in which it is expressed reflect deeply intrinsic characteristics of human sexuality.

The early European explorers were inevitably followed by the Christian missionaries. The missionaries used the same methods against the native peoples that had been used centuries before by Rome and its church to attempt to purge homosexuality from earlier European cultures. Neill writes:

Early explorers were taken aback by the casual acceptance of homosexual behavior among tribal peoples and confounded by the seemingly universal presence of androgynous homosexual individuals, whom they often found playing important leadership roles in many tribes. Though in most cases the reaction of the other Europeans wasn't as drastic as that of the Spanish conquistadors with their Inquisition, the missionaries who later accompanied the colonists nonetheless labored industriously to enforce their European sexual morality among the natives.

If we are convinced that homosexuality was both virtually universal and unstigmatized, then the question remains: Who was doing it with whom?

As in all cultures, there would have been men whom today we would identify as gay. But what about the straight men? Neill writes:

But as in Central and South America, homosexual behavior [in North America] was not limited to sex with what Europeans considered effeminate men. Joseph Francois Lafitau, a French Jesuit missionary in early 18th-century Canada, wrote of intense and socially recognized "special friendships" among young men, which he compared to the homosexual loves of the ancient Greeks, and which he said "are instituted in almost the same manner from one end of America to the other.... They are highly ancient in their origin, highly marked in the constancy of the practice, consecrated, if I dare say as much, in the union which they create, whose bonds are as close as those of blood and nature.... They become companions in hunting, in war and in fortune; they have a right to food and lodging in each other's cabins. The most affectionate compliment that the friend can make to his friend is to give him the name of Friend." Lafitau suspected "much real vice" in these relationships, which the missionaries, he said, suppressed because of the sodomy they associated with them.

A peculiar sickness of our post-Christian culture is that it has exerted itself cruelly and relentlessly to stop men from having sex with each other. If you follow James Neill's book from culture to culture, you will find male-male sex to be pretty much ubiquitous. Everyone did it — our paleolithic (hunter-gatherer) and neolithic (early agricultural) ancestors, Greece, Rome, Persia, Scythia, China, Japan, the Islamic world, and the natives of South America, Central America, and North

America. And in all cases it was never just gay men. Straight men were doing it, too.

The native North Americans have been a particularly rich source for anthropologists, including Will Roscoe and Walter L. Williams. The Native American traditions included not only masculine warriors but also androgynous men who were thought of as a kind of greatly valued third sex. In the isolated western frontier, even the Europeans — heathenized Christians — got in on the fun as long as there were no missionaries around. Neill points out that the Kinsey study found the highest incidence of homosexual activity in remote regions of the American West. Kinsey wrote: "It is the type of homosexuality which was probably common among pioneers and outdoor men in general. Today it is found among ranchers, cattle men, prospectors, lumbermen, and farming groups in general — in groups that are virile, physically active."

Brokeback Mountain is a truer story than we may realize.

Neil writes:

A man who had worked as a logger in the early 1900s described his homosexual experiences in the camp as an understood part of the loggers' way of life. "Not one of us could be considered effeminate, neurotic or abnormal. Yet all but two engaged in homosexual activities.... The popular method, preferred by the majority, was sodomy,

*and it was in this logging camp that I was initiated into
the discomforts, adjustments and ecstasies of this form of
sexual activity."*

All this is hard for today's gay men to even imagine
— the possibility of unconflicted sex, love, and friendship with straight men as well as with gay men. But
our male ancestors who never came in contact with
Christian puritanism actually had what we want and
what we need. They didn't have to hide their male-male
loves. They didn't have to try to be, or pretend to be,
something that they could not be. Far from being
devalued, gay men were often esteemed for their difference. If they were attracted to a straight man and played
their cards well, they just might have that man. Our gay
ancestors had their own rituals, their own roles, their
own stories, and their own rites of passage. They didn't
have to grow up and discover at adolescence — or even
younger — that they were going to have a hard life in
which they'd have to struggle to find love and support.

Before we leave the subject of what anthropology can tell us about ourselves, I should mention that
James Neill points out that most of the anthropological research on homosexuality did not begin until the
1970s, after the start of the sexual revolution. Before
that, homosexuality was a forbidden subject that was
largely ignored except in sodomy law, theology, and
psychiatry. For some truly horrifying reading, check

out Richard von Krafft-Ebing's *Psychopathia Sexualis*, first published in 1886. Krafft-Ebing was a psychiatrist. His view of homosexuality as pathological held for most of the 20th Century, until in 1974 the American Psychological Association took the position that homosexuality per se is not a mental disorder.

Though Krafft-Ebing's views on homosexuality are now obsolete, his views on morality and Christian doctrine still prevail. Just listen to Krafft-Ebing:

Christianity raised the union of the sexes to a sublime position by making woman socially the equal of man [but only socially!] and by elevating the bond of love to a moral and religious institution. Thus emanates the fact that the love of man, if considered from the standpoint of advanced civilization, can only be of a monogamic nature and must rest upon a stable basis.... In comparing the various stages of civilization it becomes evident that, despite periodic relapses, public morality has made steady progress, and that Christianity is the chief factor in this advance. We are certainly far beyond sodomitic idolatry, the public life, legislation and religious exercises of ancient Greece, not to speak of the worship of Phallus and Priapus in vogue among the Athenians and Babylonians, or the Bacchanalian feasts of the Romans and the privileged position held by the courtesans of those days.... The episodes of moral decay always coincide with the progression of effeminacy, lewdness and luxuriance of the nations.

Until progress was made in psychology, and before new anthropological research became available, gay people really had no alternatives but to face the terrible things that were said about us by "experts" such as Krafft-Ebing. When I started college in 1967, I explored the college library for books on homosexuality. I found only two categories: theology and some sickening books written by psychiatrists. Since then, we have indeed come a long way in our understanding of ourselves. But for most of the 20th Century, Krafft-Ebing's kind of thinking was what every young gay man had to try to live with.

My friend Jonathan Rauch has written about this discovery of the hard life ahead in *Denial: My 25 Years Without a Soul*. This is from the book's synopsis:

A young boy sitting on a piano bench realizes one day that he will never marry. At the time, this seems merely a simple, if odd, fact, but as his attraction to boys grows stronger, he is pulled into a vortex of denial. Not just for one year or even 10, but for 25 years, he lives in an inverted world, a place like a photographic negative, where love is hate, attraction is envy, and childhood never ends. He comes to think of himself as a kind of monster — until one day, seemingly miraculously, the world turns itself upright and the possibility of love floods in.

One by one, many of us do find our souls. But we also

look around us and see the misery in a world that treats us as aliens. We remember the casualties — those of us including friends and lovers who didn't make it. We want to change the world, but the path forward is not clear.

If you are convinced, so far, that the kind of world that we could live in has existed before in many times and many places, then let's think about what is holding us back from returning to a world like that in the future. Let's think about how we can throw off *all* of Krafft-Ebing's soul-destroying dogma, not just some of it.

❧ 3 ❧

The problem of identity

One way I try to keep tabs on social trends is by reading advice forums at places like Reddit. (Sometimes I even post little trial balloons, anonymously, to see what kind of reaction an idea receives.) One very common post, a post that you can find all over the Internet because it happens so often, reads like this:

"I'm a straight guy, a senior in high school. I have a girlfriend. I'm really only attracted to girls. My best friend is gay. I've known him since elementary school. I've known since junior high that he's gay. Last week we were drinking, and he asked me if he could suck my dick. He said it as though he was joking, but I've known for a long time that he would like to do something like that. I laughed it off, and we didn't do anything. But I've been thinking about it. It seems harmless enough, as long as it didn't fuck up our friendship. There might not be much in it for me, but I kind of feel like he deserves it or something. Maybe I'll like it. Should I do it? If I did, would that make me gay?"

Nearly always, the answer is the same, and it's rigidly insisted upon: Yes, that would make you gay, or maybe bi.

No male who is known to have had sex with another male is allowed to retain his straight identity. The straight male identity comes with many privileges, so it's a terrible thing to lose. We are living in an age of identity.

I don't want to get sidetracked here into a discussion of when and why the gay identity was invented. There's plenty of literature on that.

But it is important to note that many gay males, including young gay men, see the gay identity as an achievement. It's an identity that we accept proudly. For almost 50 years, I myself have identified as gay, and I have marched in my share of gay pride parades. But we also have to be open to a tough question: Are there ways in which identity politics is holding us back?

I know of several elderly gay men who were in the military when they were young. Elderly gay men often say that it was very common back then for guys to masturbate together or to jack each other off. "We didn't know it was gay," one such elderly man told me. "We just thought it was fun."

Though such statements from older gay men are anecdotally common, I can't prove, or quantify, that casual male-male sex became less common after men began to universally identify as gay or straight. Certainly Alfred Kinsey, working in the 1920s, 1930s, and 1940s, found male-male sex to be quite common. Nevertheless, I believe that the gay identity — essential though it was to decades of progress — has put a social and sexual barrier between gay men and straight men that formerly did not exist. Consequently I believe that many straight guys today decline to do what they would have willingly done (usually secretly) in the years before everyone was required to have a sexual identity.

I also believe (though I cannot prove it or quantify it) that "fag bashing" used to be less common. It's not so much a sexual overture that straight men resent. It's the threat to their sexual identity that terrifies them, or the implication that they too are gay unless they react aggressively to the overture.

Homophobia today, I would argue, is largely a consequence — the dark shadow, if you will — of the gay identity. The desire for male-male sex may be conscious (or not), but the identity is terrifying. Research has shown how closely homophobia is related to homosexual attraction.

Even my straight best friend (he'll come up again later), whose non-homophobic attitude is exemplary and state of the art, had some misunderstandings about gay men that I felt it was my duty to explain to him.

For example, I was with my straight friend at a large political meeting, and I noticed that a man whom I knew to be gay couldn't take his eyes off my friend and was following us as covertly as possible, mesmerized by my friend's good looks. I didn't know the gay guy very well, but it seemed to me that the merciful thing to do was to introduce him to my straight friend. (OK — maybe I had an ulterior motive: Sorry, but this straight guy is taken.)

Anyway, my straight friend had no inkling of what had just happened beneath the surface, and when I explained it to him, my friend expressed some concern that the gay guy might have thought him to be gay.

"It's not like that," I said. "When a gay guy admires you, it's because he thinks you're hot, not because he thinks you're gay. I promise you he knows you're straight."

That's the identity issue, you see. Even the most unhomophobic straight guy in the world, a straight guy with a gay best friend, values and seeks to defend his straight identity. There is nothing wrong with that. None of us who value our identity likes for others to misconstrue it.

My view is that the gay identity — which inevitably

gave rise to the reactionary straight identity — is now holding us back, though in the early decades of gay liberation it helped us to make progress.

It's time to thank the gay identity for all it has done for us and then to retire it. In retiring it, we return to the way things were before the gay identity was invented (or socially constructed, if you prefer that terminology).

That would be a world in which there is only one male sexuality — male sexuality — a world in which males have a lot of sex with each other, though some more than others. Sometimes it's secretive, and sometimes it's not. Sometimes love is involved, and sometimes it's not. It's a world in which male-male sex is no more stigmatized than masturbation. In fact male-male sex might even be *less* stigmatized than masturbation. Because every guy wants to be hot, desired, and gotten off, and all guys see it as a bit loserly to do it alone.

✂ 4 ✂

The problem of
privilege and property

One of the problems of writing a little book like this is to figure out how personal one should be. Sure, a lot of what forms our attitudes, our beliefs, our hopes and our dreams is not personal, and it's easy to talk about. But much of what makes us who we are is deeply personal. The personal usually remains private. Self-disclosure in a little book like this is particularly hard when other people are involved in our stories, because we don't want to invade others' privacy. On the matter of privilege, though, I believe I have to do a little more self-disclosure than I would like to do.

In the previous section on identity, I mentioned my straight best friend. He's young and attractive. He's developing a reputation as a writer. I've done my best to get used to the fact that other people like him a lot and that he's in demand. I'll call him Kirk. An old friend of mine generously offered to host a book party for Kirk. As a book party, the occasion was very successful.

But my old friend knew an eligible young woman whom she wanted to introduce to Kirk. My old friend, of course, knows that I'm gay, that Kirk is straight, and that I love Kirk. This old friend has impeccable gay-friendly credentials and, as a therapist, she has worked with many gay people and gay couples. Still, she failed to anticipate that setting Kirk up with a young woman with me present to witness it might be hard on me.

As it all unfolded like a bad dream, I did my best to hide my pain. I didn't say anything. It didn't come up until a week later, when Kirk told me at breakfast that the young woman had emailed him with an invitation to go hiking. He saw the look on my face.

"What?" he said.

It all came pouring out. I said that it was the most suffocating display of heterosexual privilege that I had ever experienced. I said that the young woman had completely monopolized him and stood (or sat) next to him at every moment except when he was giving his talk. She was seated next to him at the table. I was seated diagonally across, my relationship with Kirk unacknowledged. *She* was with him. I said that he had hardly spoken to me during the entire event except for when he asked me to go to the car and get another box of books. I said that I felt invisible, that I felt devalued, that I felt jealous. I said that I was greatly offended by her unconscious assumption of entitlement and privilege, as though the handsome young writer had been handed to her on the half shell. I said that no one had ever set me up with anyone, that no relationship of mine had ever been fêted or made a fuss of at a party. I said that it was painful that some privileged people could so instantly and easily get — indeed have handed to them — what I would have to work for years for but still probably not get. I said that, even worse, I had never felt such a social duty to fade into the background while someone else's aspirations for relationship were made a fuss of. I said that I had no choice but to suck it up because I had no right to make others uncomfortable simply because I was.

I believe Kirk's head was in his hands as all this poured out of me. In Kirk's defense, he did not make a fuss over her at the party, though he said he was enjoying the attention. She made a fuss over him. Everything that was suffocating about the display of heterosexual privilege had to do with her behavior and her blindness to other dynamics in the room. And I felt betrayed by my old friend, who had set them up while I was invisible.

As we talked it through, I mentioned Kirk's girl-friends from out of town who had come to visit, and how I felt that they acknowledged and respected our relationship, and how that made a world of difference.

Kirk pointed out how those girlfriends were older and more experienced and that the young woman at the party was pretty young. That's reasonable.

Kirk deflected her invitation to go hiking, by the way, giving other reasons (such as how far away she lived). But I believe he did it as a kindness to me.

Minorities who have had to struggle for justice and equality are all too aware of privilege. But those who possess unearned privileges rarely see those privileges unless they make an effort to see them. The matter of privilege is heavily entangled with identity and the politics of identity. When those with a minority identity and (consequently) a shortage of privileges push back, there is often conflict and misunderstanding. Though I would not say that the question of privilege is altogether a zero-sum affair, there nevertheless are situations in which some people must relinquish some privileges in the interest of justice and fairness.

This brings me to another awkward problem in writing a little book like this. I don't wish to criticize feminism or feminist politics. I want to live in a world in which women are strong, and equal, and in which women's grievances can be put right. But there are some things with which I must take issue. Feminism sees *men*, not women, as the privileged sex. In many ways, that is true. Clearly men have more than their share of the power and more than their share of income, for just two examples.

But there are some areas in which the privilege of women exceeds the privilege of men. One of those areas is power in the sexual marketplace. The very concept may offend us, but the sexual marketplace is real.

In our post-pagan culture, women have a monopoly on sex with men. This is a new development in human cultures. It's a consequence of the prohibition on male-male sex. Even a casual reading of some Greek and Roman history will show that, before the Christian era, women did not have a monopoly on sex with men. The mechanisms that enforce this monopoly are all around us, in the forms of carrots as well as sticks.

The sticks we're all familiar with. The carrots are less obvious. One of the carrots is the Romantic myth.

How did it come to be, for example, that when a man proposes marriage to a woman, he is expected to abase himself by going down on his knees and begging? If the woman accepts, she must be given some gold and a jewel. What are traditions like that supposed to teach us?

No doubt you've seen the stories on the Internet that I have seen — that there is one thing for which most women will refuse to date or marry a man. That's if he has had sex with men. In 2016, a poll of 1,000 women by Glamour magazine found that 63 percent of the women surveyed said that they would not date a man who has slept with another man. It's also a double standard, because the same poll found that a similar 63 percent of women rejected — for themselves — identity labels such as "heterosexual," "homosexual," and "bisexual." A man who has had sex with men (unless he can keep it secret) can expect to be damaged in the heterosexual marketplace. Perhaps this is slowly changing. I hope so.

Even if there is no sex, a straight man who marries usually will be expected to give up gay friends. I lost a friend that way even though he had been my best friend for 25 years. A new wife demanded that he get rid of me, and he did.

In another case, a straight-identified man with whom I'd been having sex regularly for nine years got married. I was a secret, but his wife found our emails. She demanded that he dump me. In that case, I understand the order to dump me. But I still can wish that the world didn't have to be that way.

When straight men and gay men are intimate — whether or not they have sex — in our post-pagan world, all too often, there are problems with wives and girlfriends. Gay men are not privileged, and even straight men do not have the unquestioned privilege of having gay friends.

A little Googling will reveal that many women even resent it when their boyfriends (or husbands) masturbate. Is that fair?

Women and feminists have been nervous about pornography for a long time. Sex tech — robots, dolls, and other developing forms of sexual alternatives for the straight male — also are increasingly arousing concerns among women. Some feminists have called for female sex robots to be banned. Why?

Male sexuality is male sexuality. In many ways, straight male sexuality and testosterone — even the boisterousness of boys — have been pathologized in some feminist thought. But female sexuality and male sexuality are very different things. And obviously I don't think there is anything wrong with men and their natural sexualities.

Closely related to the matter of sexual privilege is the matter of sexual property.

In *Dirt, Sex & Greed: Sexual Ethics in the New Testament and Their Implications for Today*, L. William Countryman goes well beyond the matter of privilege to property. In Judaism in particular, a woman was seen as the sexual property of a patriarch. Pagan arrangements sometimes involved the idea of sexual property, particularly where women were involved. The taint of property rights remains invisibly entangled in our notions about the sexual marketplace today.

A milder but just as problematic form of sexual property is the idea that some people have sexual claims on other people. A married man believes himself to have a claim on having sex with his wife. That's a sexual claim on another person. Boyfriends believe in similar sexual claims on women they're dating. A married woman makes it clear that she will not tolerate "infidelity" by her husband, and vice versa. Those are sexual claims. Few people would argue with these claims.

Our sexual claims on each other frequently come up in our stories — novels, television shows, and films. There was even a gay version of it in a sitcom recently.

In the British sitcom "Vicious," in which Ian McKellen and Derek Jacobi play an elderly gay couple, a handsome and straight young man played by Iwan Rheon becomes part of the family. In one of the episodes, another straight man is trying to endear himself to the older guys. The Iwan Rheon character puts a stop to it, in a funny scene in which he basically tells the newcomer to get lost, that these two old gay guys are taken.

That could be dismissed as merely a fantasy of older gay men. But such things have been known to happen, and elite older men such as Ian McKellan have probably witnessed it more than once. It is thoroughly Athenian. The attraction is mutual, whether there is age symmetry or not. There is competition for the best partners, because it is, after all, a marketplace.

But what's always overlooked is that, once we acknowledge that human beings can have legitimate sexual claims on other human beings, then we are on a slippery slope. Sexual claims, should anyone care to press the issue, quickly starts looking like an economic system of sexual goods that are owed to us by other people, and sexual goods that we owe to others. We unthinkingly regard our sexualities as our own private property. But our sexual claims on each other change all that. Our sexualities can be shared or restricted property, though we never stop to think of it that way.

As I said, that's a slippery slope. Because if people can have legitimate claims on other people's sexualities, then where do the claims end?

A right-wing libertarian, no doubt, would say the same thing about sexuality that he says about his money or his land: It's mine, and you have no claim on my money or my land unless I willingly enter into a contract with you.

But does that attitude make for the best of all possible worlds? Let me lead you further down the slippery slope.

Should Medicare and Medicaid pay for Viagra? As a sex-positive liberal, my view would be: Sure! Paying for Viagra for people who are elderly or poor amounts to acknowledging that people we don't even know can have legitimate claims on society for greater sexual happiness, at our expense.

In section 6 of this little book, on sexual generosity, you'll meet a young man who believed that I had a sexual claim on him, because I wasn't getting any sex one summer even though I deserved it. In this case, I never made any such claim on him (or even thought of it). But that's how he felt. I greatly admire him for it. I like people like him much more than I like right-wing libertarians and their no-trespassing signs. The world would be a much better place if there were more people like that young man.

The slippery slope is leading me toward sexual communism, isn't it? If so, I make no apologies, if the term sexual communism describes a tribal, sex-positive environment like the environment in which human sexualities developed and if everyone's sexual happiness matters. Much has been written about sexual communism, actually. I am not advocating anything as contrived as the sexual utopias imagined by the Frenchman Charles Fourier in the 19th Century, or by the old Oneida community in the United States. Such communities don't seem to work. But their goals, and their social critiques, have much to recommend them.

Communal sexual utopias, insofar as they have been tried, seem to fail for the same reason that cults in general fail, and those reasons have nothing to do with sex — authoritarian leadership, internal dissent, hierarchy problems, lack of economic viability, etc. I am not arguing for communitarian sexual utopias, if only because communal living does not appeal to me. But I am arguing for throwing off theologies (such as Augustine's) and myths (such as the Romantic myth). I'm arguing for rethinking troubling questions of privilege, property, fairness, and justice. I'm arguing for a broader and more natural view of male sexuality and male bonding.

I'm also pointing out the inequality in the marketplace. Gay men are almost completely disempowered in making sexual claims on other people. Our claims can never extend beyond the 2 percent of our own kind. We are shut out of the larger market, leading to a kind of sexual poverty. We are surrounded by vast riches in the form of beautiful men radiating masculinity. We see them every day. But 98 percent of those men are beyond our reach, because we are poor. We are the lowest caste in the sexual marketplace.

My interest, I should emphasize, is not in social theory, sexual politics, or dogma. This book came about only because I have asked myself why my life — and the lives of men I have known, both gay and straight — were on the whole so sexually unhappy. I wanted to understand how things came to be the way they are, why it didn't have to be that way, and how it might be otherwise.

❧ 5 ❧

The problem of symmetry

In addition to identity, privilege, and property, another matter that is deeply and invisibly entangled in our system of sexual ethics is the matter of symmetry.

Our society is highly suspicious of any relationship that isn't symmetrical. There are a few exceptions, of course — parent-child, or student-teacher relationships are not expected to be symmetrical. But our marriages, our friendships, and our sexual affiliations are expected to be symmetrical. Our lovers are expected to be of a similar age, similar socioeconomic class, and even similar degrees of attractiveness. These rules apply fairly consistently to both gay and straight (or mixed) relationships.

If you point this out to someone and ask why this might be, the most thoughtful answer you might get is that it's about power. We frown on relationships in which one person has more power than the other, because that implies exploitation. Most of the time, symmetry is probably a good social value. But that doesn't mean that asymmetrical relationships are always bad.

These days, if you point out that the *eromenos-erastês* male-male relationships of classical Greece probably had their roots in pedagogical arrangements inherited from even older societies (akin to apprentice-ships), then you run the risk of advocating pederasty, which I am not advocating (though I would encourage everyone to become familiar with what anthropology has to say about age asymmetry). Where male-male sex is involved, there is a particular tendency toward age asymmetry, both now and back then. In spite of what we know about the Greeks, gay culture today has as-similated the ideal of symmetry from our puritan op-pressors. Every gay marriage that I have ever heard of has been highly symmetrical.

But if my straight best friend was 27 when I met him, and I was 60, is that a problem? I am happy to report that no one I know seems to see it that way, including the rural Republicans in this county. Everyone im-mediately saw the basis of our friendship — our in-tellectual compatibility, our common interests such as reading, writing books, simple living, and having a garden and orchard and chickens. We are two peas in a pod, in spite of the age difference. In fact, people naturally seemed to assume right from the start, unjudgmentally but wrongly, that we were lovers.

If it's true that straight men devalue older women, then it's also true that gay men devalue older men. But gay men *don't* devalue older women, and straight men don't devalue older men. I suspect that these are natural traits wired into our male sexualities and that these natural traits are somehow connected to age asymmetry. The most important mentor of my life was an older woman. That probably would be rare with straight men.

Symmetry is related to *reciprocity*. Sexual relationships that are asymmetrical also are likely to be sexually unreciprocal.

If there is age symmetry in a relationship between a gay male and a straight male, then the straight guy feels an obligation toward sexual reciprocity. He knows that's something that he can't very well offer. But in an age-asymmetrical friendship, if sex does happen (it often does), then the sex is not reciprocal. I think it's best to leave that unexplained.

The 19th Century sexual communist Charles Fourier, with purely heterosexual arrangements in mind, encouraged younger people to offer themselves to older people in the interest of maximizing sexual happiness for all. There's a hint of this from the Greek historian Diodorus Siculus, who wrote that young Celtic men would offer themselves to older men and would be insulted if the offer was refused. In my novel *Fugue in*

Ursa Major, I made a joke about this, as though it is a kind of sexual Social Security — pay in when you're young, get it back when you're old. Frankly I think most young men (women, too?) would sign up for that idea, if the old-age pension was adjusted for sexual orientation.

Ours is a sexual ethic and sexual culture that encourages stinginess and abstinence. It tolerates and perpetuates gross imbalances of privilege. It still contains patriarchal elements of sexual property. Our sexual ethic requires that 2 percent (or so) of the male population keep their gay paws off the other 98 percent of the male population, those who are richest in the masculinity that the 2 percent crave.

Some may ask why, in writing about sexual grievances, I have not mentioned male sexual privilege, or male sexual violence, or rape. That's because I don't know anything about those issues. They have not touched my life. I leave those issues to those who *do* know something about them, just as they have left my grievances to me.

ᴄᴖ **6** ᴖᴄ

Sexual generosity

In the previous section I mentioned sexual stinginess. Its opposite is sexual generosity.

Our sexual marketplace, with its Tinder, its Grindr, its craigslist (does anybody still use craigslist?) does an efficient job of matching equal trades for symmetrical sex. But we don't have any social custom of asymmetrically matching those in need with those who might be willing to be sexually generous. Lacking the custom, we lack the idiom. We lack the categories. "Men seeking men," or "women seeking men," is about as far as our categories go.

I have never seen ads like these imaginary ads. Have you?

M4W: Heavy guy, gamer, moderately autistic, age 23, still a virgin, seeks young lady for mercy sex.

M4W: VGL college rower, 6'1", 175, will satisfy lonely widow, 60+, strictly NSA, washer and dryer optional.

M4MW: Fully functional bi male, 55, athletic, offers anonymous proxy services for elderly married couple coping with ED. You call the shots.

We all know what we want and what we are looking for, but rarely do we perceive another person's sexual need. Even in relationships, this is a problem. It's why Dan Savage invented the 3G's for sexual relationships: Be good, giving, and game.

I'd like to mention two cases of male-male sexual generosity.

When I was 27, I spent the summer at an artists' community in rural Massachusetts. I was the only gay male there. It was a lonely time for me. Everybody was having lots of sex but me. This was in Cummington, Massachusetts, and the straight folk and lesbians called the place "Cumming tons." One chilly July night, well after dark, I was sitting alone by the fireplace. There was a very handsome 17-year-old young man (age 16 makes you legal in Massachusetts) who was there from Georgia to spend the summer with his father, who was a sculptor. The young man came and sat down with me, and we talked. After a while, he invited me to go for a walk. We ended up in an old cemetery, the cemetery, in fact, that William Cullen Bryant (whose mansion is still nearby) had in mind when he wrote the poem "Thanatopsis." The night was cool and damp, and this handsome young man stopped by his room to get a blanket. As we walked and talked, he offered to share the blanket with me, hanging from our shoulders like a cape. With a remarkable innocence and directness, he offered himself to me, like a Celtic boy to an older Greek. He felt sorry for me, he said, because I was the only person there who didn't have someone to have sex with. (He was having regular sex with a young woman who worked in the children's center.) We went back to his room. He was inexperienced, but not only was he good, giving, and game, he also had a beautiful body.

Though at age 27 I was no ogre, I've often wondered how this young man achieved such an advanced state of consciousness. I'm often tempted to believe that, in the terminology of the physicist Roger Penrose, it's a "non-computable Platonic value" that's just out there in the ether, like music and mathematics, to those who can attune to it. Or maybe it was because my young benefactor's parents were hippies. And he wasn't from just anywhere in Georgia, he was from Athens. Sometimes I remember him and wonder how his life went. Pretty well, I'd guess.

Another case of male-male sexual generosity involves a friend whom I've know for 30 years. He lives with another old friend of mine. Like many gay households, they have what we gay people call "acquired family." My friends' acquired family includes a couple of young straight men whom they've known for 25 years and who come over regularly to hang out, drink beer, watch old movies, and shoot the breeze. Every Sunday, it's their tradition for my friend (I'll call him Daniel) to cook dinner for everyone. They call it family night. One of the straight men is married, the other (I'll call him Mark) has had a series of girlfriends. Daniel loves Mark, and everyone knows it. But like most gay men in love with straight men, Daniel repressed his feelings and just tried to be a good friend to Mark.

Daniel had had a very bad year. There were some serious problems with his hearing, they were losing their rented house and were forced to move, and Daniel, a college professor, was having job problems. Then a friend who also was a longtime member of Daniel's acquired family died. Everyone was crushed, but Daniel was scraping the bottom, and everyone looked to Daniel to stay strong and to take the lead in navigating through tough times.

One Sunday evening after the family dinner, Daniel was sitting on the screen porch, alone, having a drink and thinking. Mark came out and asked him if he was OK (though Mark knew very well that Daniel was not OK).

"Come upstairs when you get a minute," Mark said.

Daniel nodded. Everyone else was downstairs in the living room, watching an old movie.

When Daniel went upstairs, Mark was standing there naked. What happened next is a private matter. But it's not difficult to guess what Mark might have been thinking. No one lives forever. Daniel has been there for me for 25 years. I know what he wants, and it's cruel of me not to give it to him. And now is the time, because I've never seen Daniel, normally so strong, so crushed.

The saddest part of this story, to me, is that it took 25 years. Yes, gay men can handle that, if they love you. I was in love with a best friend for 25 years, too, though that moment of generosity never came. The opportunity was lost, because a new wife expected him to dump me, which he did.

There is something biblical about so much love and waiting. Jacob was so much in love with Rachel that he worked seven years to be able to marry her. But after the seven years, Rachel's father tricked Jacob and demanded that Jacob work another seven years to have Rachel. That makes 14 years, a biblical record that many gay men can beat.

Seven years — not to mention 14 years — is presented as an eternity and an exemplary proof of love in the Bible. But to gay men who love straight men, it is nothing.

Gay men have a reputation for being highly promiscuous. During the AIDS era, it was common to hear that some urban gay men had hundreds of sex partners per year. I don't doubt the truth of that. In San Francisco I certainly knew some men who were in that category.

But extremes of promiscuity mask the misery and isolation of others. I have a friend — a very handsome friend, I might add, who is constantly hit on by both men and women — who didn't have sex for 17 years after his first lover broke his heart.

Why have I written a section on sexual generosity and unrequited sexual longing? It's because I — and many of my friends who also have tried to live for love — have endured levels of hopelessness that no straight person would ever put up with. Straight men and women would just move on. They have more options.

I don't want to get too far off the ground here into biblical levels of deprivation and Jane Eyre levels of romanticism. But I do believe that there is — or at least that there can be — something strangely rare and Platonic about the gay heart when it is in love. Why can't we just move on? I don't know. But I do know that we pay a heavy price for it. As Edna St. Vincent Millay wrote, "Many a man is making friends with death even as I speak, for lack of love alone."

Not only is this all around us today — as Michael Hobbes' article showed — it has been going on for hundreds of years.

If you're thinking of composing a craigslist ad to help out someone in need, could you let me know? I have a little list.

∽ 7 ∽

Did prisons save the world from Oscar Wilde?

A bunch of authoritarians have been telling us for far too long what we can and cannot do. The methods they use to control male sexuality (for our own good, of course) have changed from century to century. Looking back into history, it's easy to recognize prudes and puritans for what they are. In the present, it can be more difficult. Prudes and puritans always frame their prohibitions in a way that makes them appear to be on the leading edge of social progress.

This is from a handbook for boys published in 1909 (*From Youth Into Manhood*, Winfield S. Hall). It's about the terrible things that masturbation will do to you:

So with the one who has broken Nature's laws in the sin of masturbation, Nature punishes him by removing, step by step, his manhood. This is brought about in a very natural way, easy to understand.... As this act is repeated from week to week, or as in some extreme cases, every day or two, the youth feels the foundations of his manhood undermined. He notes that his muscles are becoming more and more flabby; that his back is weak; his eyes may after a time become sunken and "fishy," his hands clammy; he is unable to look anybody straight in the eye. As the youth becomes conscious of his weakness, he loses confidence, refuses to take part in athletic sports; avoids the company of his young women friends; and becomes a non-entity in the athletic and social life of the community.

Here is a more modern version. It was written by Orson Scott Card (the science fiction writer) in 1990:

Laws against homosexual behavior should remain on the books, not to be indiscriminately enforced against anyone who happens to be caught violating them, but to be used when necessary to send a clear message that those who flagrantly violate society's regulation of sexual behavior cannot be permitted to remain as acceptable, equal citizens within that society. The goal of the polity is not to put homosexuals in jail. The goal is to discourage people from engaging in homosexual practices in the first place, and, when they nevertheless proceed in their homosexual behavior, to encourage them to do so discreetly, so as not to shake the confidence of the community in the polity's ability to provide rules for safe, stable, dependable marriage and family relationships.

On what grounds does Orson Scott Card believe that male-male sex is so dangerous to the "community" that it should be forbidden by law? As far as I can tell, it's because Card, a Mormon, believes that "our Lord" says so. Card, an authoritarian, wants rules and regulations on sexual behavior ostensibly to protect marriage and society. But marriage and society are institutions, not people. That an institution might cause more misery than it alleviates does not occur to Card. He wants to retain the threat of prison "to send a clear message." How'd that work out with Oscar Wilde? But if you look at the real threats to "safe, stable, dependable marriage," they are threats that Card does not bother to call out and preach against. Here (from Googling) are some *actual* causes of unstable marriages and divorce that Card has never inveighed against, as far as I know:

- Lack of commitment
- Too much arguing
- Heterosexual infidelity
- Marrying too young
- Lack of equality
- Abuse
- Money problems
- Differences in libido

- Children from previous relationships
- Intrusive parents
- Addiction
- Dwindling intimacy
- Laziness
- Unmet expectations

I well understand why conservatives are concerned about the stability of their form of marriage. Divorce is hell. Children pay a horrible price when the relationships of heterosexual couples end. But conservatives never ask themselves whether their idea of marriage is part of the problem, not the solution. The Celts, under Brehon law, had 10 different degrees of marriage. Celtic children had many adults to depend on, not just two. Why must we unquestioningly assume that a new definition of marriage developed by Christian theologians somehow contains more wisdom than the customs of the old Celts?

Orson Scott Card does make a point that I happen to agree with. He writes, "... When they nevertheless proceed in their homosexual behavior, to encourage them to do so discreetly." I wholeheartedly agree. *Straight guys don't have to tell.* Some gay guys will disagree with me. They seek to shame those who are not "out." But I would argue that there is no shame in being secretive or discreet about male-male sex as long as we live in a society that will misunderstand you and punish you for it. Of course it's true that millions of gay people "coming out" has been a major factor — probably the biggest factor — in how attitudes have changed in recent decades. But people should come out when they want to come out, and no one has a right to "out" others. An exception to this would be outing a politician who hypocritically uses the powers of public office to harm gay people, while secretly having gay sex.

In the final stages of writing this book, I did a Google search to check for recent material that I might have missed. I came across an article in the British version of GQ magazine with this headline: *The straight men dating men and the gay men who fall in love with them.* The article is dated March 2017. Like me, this article defends straight men's right to secrecy, if that's their choice. The author of the article, Justin Myers, writes, "[B]ecause increased tolerance cuts both ways, ... it's just as wrong to call somebody out for not adopting the label of gay as it is to criticise someone who does."

I believe that it is both ethically and strategically wrong for gay men to slam straight men when they break the gay-straight barrier but refuse to accept the label "gay" or "bi." It is ethically wrong because it violates two of their rights: the right to choose their own identity, and the right to take part in harmless and consensual sexual behavior. It is wrong strategically because the more straight guys who are doing it, the better. Over the long term, this is one of the things that change our culture. We gay men should be the last people on earth to infringe on the sexual freedom of straight men, even if the privileges of straight identity open doors for them that are closed to gay men.

You think I'm radical? How about this:

Tom Ford, the movie director, told GQ magazine that he believes all men should be penetrated and fucked. "You shouldn't force yourself to do it. But it's really not that different than having a massage. It doesn't feel that much different. It's skin. You should do it with someone you like. Do it with a friend who you think is great. It's very easy. It's normal."

Ford's reasons are not exactly the reasons that I would give, but I appreciate his perspective: "I think it would help them understand women. It's such a vulnerable position to be in, and it's such a passive position to be in. And there's such an invasion, in a way, that even if it's consensual, it's just very personal. And I think there's a psyche that happens because of it that makes you understand and appreciate what women go through their whole life, because it's not just sexual, it's a complete setup of the way the world works, that one sex has the ability to literally—and is expected to and is wanted to — but also there's an invasion. And I think that that's something most men do not understand at all."

Ford is talking about breaking down binary constructions that are bound up in our identities. Some of those binaries are: Male-female, gay-straight, active-passive, dominant-submissive, top-bottom, agent-object. *All* of these binaries are blurry, including the male-female binary. I would argue that nature is incapable of producing a human psyche in which these opposites are not blurred. They are always blended. It must be exhausting to be a straight male who feels compelled to always be dominant, always the active one, always the top, always an agent rather than an object.

Sex is a powerful form of human bonding. It's a social glue developed by nature. In all things, nature bats last. The bonding power of sex is much more powerful than human social inventions such as marriage contracts or theologies like Augustine's. And whether we approve or not, the bonding power of sex almost never lasts a lifetime, hence the Celts' 10 different degrees of marriage. We've learned that vast efforts of repression, stigma, surveillance, policing, and misery are required to keep a puritan system in place. The problem is not that the social structures that Orson Scott Card defends are decaying and failing. The problem is that those social structures were invented and imposed on us in the first place. It was inevitable that we would eventually throw them off.

I actually used to be friends with Orson Scott Card,

back in the 1980s. He told me once that we fail to realize, at our peril, that our social structures are a delicate ecology evolved from the wisdom of our ancestors. He said that, if we change something with the intent of making it better (for example, tolerating male-male sex), then we run the risk of damaging our social structures in unpredictable ways. Don't go around breaking things, Card advises. Trust the wisdom of our ancestors.

That's interesting, and no doubt there's a great deal of truth in it. But Card doesn't see how he's defeated by his own argument.

The old pagan societies, now exterminated, had social structures that evolved from the wisdom of *their* ancestors. It was a much older wisdom than puritan wisdom. It can be traced back for millennia to our tribal days. It was Card's theologians who meddled and broke things.

∽ 8 ∽

Straight guys
don't come easy

The wisest words I ever heard from a gay man are from James Leo Herlihy (1927-1993), a novelist and author of *Midnight Cowboy*. He said, *Don't look for a lover, be one.*

No joke, I have done my best to try to live my gay life according to Herlihy's advice. Have I always been happy? Of course not. Have I often been lonely? Of course. But I believe that, if I had spent my time desperately looking for a lover, with little regard for what I have to offer *as* a lover, then my life probably would have gone on the rocks, and I'd be a dark statistic today instead of a contented old man.

But I would like to offer a corollary of Herlihy's advice, based on my experience. It's this: *Don't look for a friend, be one.*

What's the difference between a friend and a lover?

Is it sex? Not necessarily! Sex between friends can be very sweet and satisfying, and without a lot of the freight.

Friends often last longer than lovers. When lovers stay together, it's usually because they're friends.

We are all immersed in the romantic myth. We want to be swept off our feet, adored, desired, and live happily ever after in a perpetual state of limerance.

I have never known a single person, gay or straight, for whom the romantic myth came true. We might think we're living the myth for a little while, and there is no greater bliss on earth, while it lasts. But soon the limerance will subside, right on schedule. Odds are, one or both of you will start looking for a new lover.

Why am I telling you this?

This is a book about straight men and gay men, so the hard truth that I'm trying to soften is that no straight man will ever be your lover. But he might well be your *friend.*

This hard truth trips us up so often that it's a cliché in online forums: "Help! I'm in love with my straight best friend!"

When gay guys get into this situation and ask for help online, the advice they get is pretty consistent and pre-dictable: Don't go there. It can never work. Move on. No he won't have sex with you. Stick with your own kind. Check yourself for internalized homophobia.

I disagree with this advice. There's no denying that it's often true, but it doesn't *have* to be that way. Much depends on who you are and how you play your cards. Some rules must be broken. But some rules must be obeyed.

If you play it as a friendship, then there is hope. If you are as aware of what your straight friend wants from you as you are aware of what you want from him, then there is hope.

If I didn't believe that close friendships between gay men and straight men are instinctive and natural and healthy, then I would not have written this little book.

But your task is very similar to the task of the straight guy who declines to be constrained by the straight identity. You must look back to a more pagan time when there was no such thing as the romantic myth. Friendship is enough. Face it: What the romantic myth teaches gay guys to long for is like what every straight young woman is taught to long for. She's a princess. Her prince will come along and sweep her off her feet. The prince swears eternal admiration and eternal passion. Her prince's ardor is so great that he rips off her bodice and takes her — before the wedding. The wedding costs $30,000. It's in a church. (Why is that?) They make vows that they will never break (until they do). She dances with her prince. At midnight, they wave goodbye to their friends and retreat to their bower, where they live happily ever after, complete unto themselves except insofar as children and making a living intrude slightly on their bliss.

I believe that the romantic myth is one of the worst cruelties ever imposed on human beings, the adult version of the Santa Claus fraud inflicted on children. Eventually children must learn that there is no Santa Claus.

The book *Getting the Love You Want,* first published in 1988, has sold more than 2 million copies. But since 1988, the marriage rate has steadily declined as marriage becomes increasingly unpopular and impractical. If people are getting the love they want, then the book isn't helping people to get it through marriage. I haven't read this book. But I do note that the title is about *getting* what you want, not about what you can offer others. That's our consumption-based culture. We're supposed to be able to go out there and get what we want. The Internet and its apps have further aggravated things. Grindr and Tinder are all about shopping for what *you* want.

Let's compare classical Athens. We have a good record of that, thanks to writer-philosophers such as Plato. In Plato's *Symposium*, there is a long discussion about when it is proper for a *beloved* to *gratify* his *lover*. Note the asymmetry between lover and beloved. Like girlfriends and boyfriends today, lovers and beloveds then were guided by scripts and templates. For an attractive young man, finding his older lover was like falling off a log. Once a lover finds such a young man to love, the lover will know what is expected of him. The lover will know what privileges he stands to gain. He will know what maintenance will be required. And the beloved knows that, at the right time, the lover must be gratified.

To *gratify* means, coarsely translated, to put out. Every young Greek knew that a worthy lover was entitled to sex, though how long he had to work for it depended upon how worthy he was.

We need not venture too far here into Greek social institutions. I only wish to show that the pagans had these institutions. Plato's *Symposium* and the *Phaedrus* are good reading on this subject.

Roman institutions and social templates were not as high-minded as the Greek, though they were not always as abased as slavery, either. Biblical scholars believe that a gay Roman centurion and his boy even appear in the Bible. The centurion seeks Jesus out (Matthew 8:5 and Luke 7:1) and pleads with Jesus to heal his *pais*, who is very sick and very dear to the centurion. The King James translation and other translations use the word "servant" for *pais*. But the Greek word, *pais*, scholars say, almost always has a sexual connotation. And Roman soldiers often kept a boy.

The pagan culture that fascinates me most, because DNA testing shows me to be genetically Celtic, is Celtic culture. I want to know how my ancestors lived. I want to understand what Rome and the church did to them. In section 5 of this book, the section on symmetry, I mention how the Greek historian Diodorus Siculus wrote about Celtic youths offering themselves to strangers. Though much knowledge of early Celtic life has been wiped out by Roman imperialism, what we do know is intriguing. Celtic culture seems to have pulled off a twofer that the church found altogether intolerable — the empowerment of women *and* so much male-male sex that even the Greeks took notice. Children were cherished and were heavily invested in. A portion of the land was set aside for the support of widows and the poor. As I mentioned earlier, the Brehon law recognized 10 different degrees of marriage. Ten! To a puritan (Orson Scott Card, section 7), this sounds like a nightmare. But this is what the church destroyed and replaced with sexual misery for all, a cruel system of millstone marriage, with bastards and abandoned children galore. It is said that in England in 1806 there were more hangings for sodomy than for murder.

So you see, my fellow gay guys, what we are dealing with and why fixing it is not going to be easy. You also see why, today, when you fall in love with a straight guy, you're likely to get your heart broken, though an Iron Age Celt would have a sporting chance at a good friend-ship and good sex.

But let's return to James Leo Herlihy. Straight guys are not going to like you simply because you find them attractive. They're not going to put out for you just because you want them to. We have to constantly ask ourselves what we have to offer them. What we have to offer is proportional to how hard we're willing to work at *being* a lover. Or a friend.

Even the pagan Greeks had to work for it and wait for it. They had to be worthy.

Like it not, sex and relationships are a marketplace. There's always a *quid pro quo*, a this for that — a trade. Even Catholic heterosexual marriage is a *quid pro quo*, with rights, duties, and grounds for annulment.

If I'm right — that straight guys just naturally love their gay guys as much as gay guys love their straight guys — then we have to do only half the work. Straight guys, once they see that they've been had by somebody else's terrible ideas, will do the other half. I think they see us as a kind of third sex, somewhere between straight men and women. My straight best friend once referred to me as a "hybrid" gay guy, because I know how engines and other machines work and I have a lot of tools. You might worry that, if by some miracle all the straight guys in the world suddenly wanted male-male sex, then all the straight guys would start doing it with each other, and we gay guys would still be out in the cold. But I don't think so. We gay guys are different somehow, because nature made us different. We adore our straight guys more. We need them more. We're more vulnerable. We make them feel manly. Like women, we trigger their instinct to protect us. We gladly do things for them that women and other straight men won't do. We treat them like princes; straight guys treat each other likes bros. It makes them feel good when they make us happy. They're glad they're not like us, and yet they like us just the way we are.

Forbidding gay guys to love men — all men — is as cruel as forbidding women to love men. Though I love my gay friends, and though some of my gay friends and former lovers have stood by me for 40 years and longer, I cannot live in a ghetto with them.

This is not a predicament that we can fight our way out of, gay men against the world.

We have to cook up a new world with all-natural ingredients, nothing artificial, one friend at a time.

∽ 9 ∽

Why this is not radical

Many people will see my arguments in this little book as hopelessly radical. Male-male sex will never be ubiquitous and unstigmatized, some will say. For one, they'll say, straight men just won't do stuff like that (ha!). They'll say that separating sexual behavior from sexual identify is impossible. Many women will resent my message, because modern women prefer their men to be heterosexually pure, and women will want to keep a status quo in which women are the only approved object of male orgasms.

But I argue that my critics not only are wrong, but that they also have got things exactly backwards. I'm actually arguing for an *old* status quo — the way things were before the real radicals — theologians such as Augustine of Hippo — came up with radical new anti-sex rules 1,500 years ago and the church and its agents began policing our sex lives. They even taught us to police ourselves, using a system of lies that we started believing.

So-called queer theory, I would argue, is at a dead end. For example, look at Gilreath Shannon's book, *The End of Straight Supremacy: Realizing Gay Liberation*, which went over with a dull thud. Like many such books, it is largely an exercise in jargon. Its theories are conjured from the same sort of thin air from which Augustine of Hippo conjured *his* theological theories.

Compare Jane Ward's *Not Gay: Sex Between Straight White Men*. Though her critics raise questions about Ward's research, Ward does at least look at actual human behaviors, human motivations, and human instincts. She is not conjuring out of thin air; she does not lose her way in abstract theory. And, as it happens, Ward's findings lead in the same direction as my thinking. As one reviewer of her book put it, "The conclusion I drew from the book was a strong need for a push for rights for sexual behavior, regardless of any connection to identity. Ward doesn't provide any guidelines for such a political shift, but she has played an important part in laying the groundwork for a focus on sexual behavior rights."

That's the argument that I am making, and I believe that in many ways I pick up the argument where Jane Ward leaves off. I am arguing that the movement for gay rights has achieved all it can achieve (though we must constantly remain vigilant against those who still don't respect our rights). The rights that we need to be thinking about now are rights for male sexual behavior with no connection to sexual identity. I reject the idea that this is a homophobic position, that it's a position that subordinates gay men, or that it's a position that fails to appreciate the accomplishments of gay liberation. The gay rights movement was necessary. It was successful. Of course there still are battles to fight. Unfairness, injustice, and discrimination are still all too common, and we must not relent in our opposition to those things. In many ways, transsexuals are the new political scapegoats, and we gay people must use what we have learned to stand with transsexuals in their fight for equality. The fact that we still have some old battles to fight does not mean that we cannot move forward in a new direction.

But my argument is less about politics and more about how we live our lives. It's an argument not only about sex and who we have sex with. It's also an argument about love and bonding and family formation. It's an argument about male sexualities in general, not just gay sexualities.

Much of Jane Ward's research had to do with unhealthy male behaviors such as fraternity hazing. In the world that I'm imagining, these male sexual behaviors don't have to expressed in disguised, deniable, unhealthy ways. I believe that, were it not for the stigmas — particularly the stigma of the dreaded gay identity — these behaviors would be expressed in much healthier ways.

I believe that, relieved of stigma, our society would greatly benefit by returning to the old status quo of the social glue generated by male affection, male bonding, and male-male sex. For some images of what we have lost, just in the last hundred years, see books such as *Picturing Men: A Century of Male Relationships in Everyday American Photography.*

Whether you're older or younger, gay or straight, look around you. If you're reading this book, the odds are that the issues I have written about here touch your life in some way.

There are reports that young people increasingly are describing their identities as "mostly straight," acknowledging same-sex attraction and same-sex possibilities. That's an important start. It's a trend to be encouraged. The worst thing we could do would be to try to pressure these young people into picking one of the older identities.

I'm willing to venture a prediction. I believe that, generation by generation, the percentage of young men who identify as "mostly straight" will steadily increase. Eventually the day will come, I believe, when male sexual identities such as gay and straight will no longer seem necessary or useful, as was the case a few generations ago. Those of us who are living today won't be around to see that world. But even if we don't live to see that world, what's to stop us from living that way today? Just as the longest journey unfolds one step at time, this is a journey that unfolds one person at a time. Other people's hangups need not hold us back.

Religionists have made an incredibly big deal out of male-male sex. These days, only a religious fringe believes that male-male sex causes hurricanes, or that God destroys cities or nations for it. But these religious prohibitions are wired into us in all sorts of dark and insidious ways. We can't purge it from our culture — at least not for a long time. But we can see through it, make fun of it, laugh at it, and ignore it. We can stop teaching it to our children.

In the hierarchy of human needs, sex is usually placed in the third category, more important than safety. Our sexualities also are bound up with the two upper categories — esteem and self-actualization. Puritans have no qualms about making people sexually miserable. In fact, making people sexually miserable often seems to be a desirable goal of puritans. But sex and sexual happiness are much too important for us to allow other people to damage our lives. We are taught to feel shame about sex, and our feelings of shame make sex hard to talk about. It was hard for me to write and publish this little book, because I dread the shaming and the criticism that I'm in for.

But I'm not asking anyone to "come out," or to join a

movement. You don't have to agree with everything I've said. It boils down to this: Many centuries ago, some men with sick minds came up with some terrible ideas. They used those terrible ideas to threaten us and to tell us how to live. They changed the world, and not for the better.

Why don't we change the world back, one life at a time?

Years ago, I saw the rock musical "Hair" on Broadway, twice. I can't say it any better than this:

I wish every mother and father in this theater
Would go home tonight and make a speech to their teenagers
And say kids, be free, no guilt
Be whoever you are, do whatever you want to do
Just as long as you don't hurt anybody.

And you don't need to tell anybody, either.

Further reading

The Origins and Roles of Same-Sex Relations in Human Societies. James Neill. MacFarland, 2009. 470 pages.

Changing Ones: Third and Fourth Genders in Native North America. Will Roscoe. St. Martin's Griffin, 1998. 320 pages.

Spirit and the Flesh: Sexual Diversity in American Indian Culture. Walter L. Williams. Beacon Press, 1992. 368 pages.

The Celtic World. Edited by Miranda Green. Routledge, 1995. 864 pages.

The Ancient Celts. Barry Cunliffe. Oxford University Press, 1997. 324 pages.

From Shame to Sin: The Christian Transformation of Sexual Morality in Late Antiquity. Kyle Harper. Harvard University Press, 2013. 306 pages.

Dirt, Greed, and Sex: Sexual Ethics in the New Testament and Their Implications for Today. L. William Countryman. Fortress Press, 2007. 350 pages.

The Greeks and Greek Love. James Davidson. Random House, 2007. 780 pages.

Greek Homosexuality. K.J. Dover. Harvard University Press, 1989. 246 pages.

Basic Writings of Saint Augustine. Edited by Whitney J. Oates. Random House, 1948. 888 pages.

The Brehon Laws. Laurence Ginnell. Forgotten Books, 2012. 250 pages.

The Theory of the Four Movements. Charles Fourier. Cambridge University Press. 2008. 328 pages.

Not Gay: Sex Between Straight White Men. Jane Ward. New York University Press, 2015. 240 pages.

The Meaning of Human Existence. Edward O. Wilson. Liveright, 2014. 208 pages.

Sex and Marriage in Ancient Ireland. Patrick C. Power. Dufour, 1997. 96 pages.

A History of Pagan Europe. Prudence Jones. Routledge, 1997. 288 pages.

The Oxford Handbook of Late Antiquity. Scott Fitzgerald Johnson. Oxford University Press, 2012. 1,296 pages.

The Táin, from the Irish Epic Táin Bó Cuailnge. Translated by Thomas Kinsella. Oxford University Press, 1969. 282 pages.

Celts: Art and Identity. Edited by Julia Farley and Fraser Hunter for the British Museum. 304 pages.

CPSIA information can be obtained
at www.ICGtesting.com
Printed in the USA
LVOW11s0016170418
573761LV00001B/13/P